ME!

A Baby's Guide to Parenting

Newborn to 3 Years Old

JUNE P. BULLEN

iUniverse, Inc.
New York Lincoln Shanghai

ME!
A Baby's Guide to Parenting

Copyright © 2007 by June P. Bullen

All rights reserved. No part of this book may be used or reproduced by any means, graphic, electronic, or mechanical, including photocopying, recording, taping or by any information storage retrieval system without the written permission of the publisher except in the case of brief quotations embodied in critical articles and reviews.

iUniverse books may be ordered through booksellers or by contacting:

iUniverse
2021 Pine Lake Road, Suite 100
Lincoln, NE 68512
www.iuniverse.com
1-800-Authors (1-800-288-4677)

The views expressed in this work are solely those of the author and do not necessarily reflect the views of the publisher, and the publisher hereby disclaims any responsibility for them.

ISBN: 978-0-595-42051-3 (pbk)
ISBN: 978-0-595-86396-9 (ebk)

Printed in the United States of America

Contents

INTRODUCTION vii

PRE-BORN TO DELIVERY ROOM AND
BEYOND 1

FOR THE NEW PARENTS 9

NEWBORN 17

IT'S TIME TO GO HOME 21

HOME AT LAST 23

OUR FIRST OUTING 27

BABY NOT NEWBORN 31

FOUR–SIX MONTHS 33

TEETHING 35

SEVEN-NINE MONTHS 39

10–12 MONTHS OLD 41

1–2 YEARS OLD 47

THE ARRIVAL OF A SIBLING 51

2–3 YEARS OLD 53
TOILET TRAINING 55
CONCLUSION 59
HELPFUL HINTS 61
CHILDHOOD AILMENTS 67
AUTHOR BIOGRAPHY 71

INTRODUCTION

As with so many things in life, parenting is not an easy task. In fact it could be the hardest task we ever have in our lifetime. There is no blueprint to follow to ensure success, as each baby is an individual. So, what is good for one baby may not be good for another.

To help alleviate some of your doubts and insecurities, baby is going to direct you through this somewhat daunting task, by explanation from her point of view, in her easy to understand language.

As a parent, you need to happily accept that you have created a 24/7 commitment involving sleepless nights, endless washing, pacing the floor with your new baby, and seemingly nonstop feeding. It will feel like utter chaos from morning to night. There will be times when you will wonder why you decided to take on this full time responsibility, as it is hard and very tiring work with absolutely no routine or system to make it easier. But it will prove to be very worthwhile, because in time, life will settle.

A new routine will be established, sleep deprivation won't be as prevalent as the first few weeks, the bond between you and your baby will be growing by the day, and it's then you will appreciate how your baby makes you a family. A happy, connected family if your attitude is positive, and you are full of love for your new baby.

The experience of parenthood will open up all sorts of unexpected pleasures and happiness that would otherwise not have been a part of your life; and the best part is, it's for ever.

Even though the impact of a new baby in the house can be really quite traumatic for both parents, this upheaval can be lessened by sharing as many of the responsibilities as you can, and resting as much as possible when your baby is asleep. Although still important, housework, shopping and cooking should now become less of a priority than before baby arrived. Don't feel inadequate or ashamed to accept the help of family and friends, especially in the first 6–8 weeks, as this will reduce your work load, and lessen your stress levels. A happy, rested parent will provide a much more stable environment for a newborn baby, who can actually sense whether you are calm or uptight, and will probably respond accordingly.

Baby is not the only one in a strange environment. You, as parents, haven't had this experience before, so you will all be learning together.

What your child learns in the first six years of life basically determines what type of character he or she is going to be. If your child is guided, treated with love and respect, taught right from wrong, and provided with your time and attention; then he is most likely going to grow into a confident, well balanced, motivated and thoughtful human being, who will always want you to be a part of his life.

Every living being needs and welcomes unconditional love. Think how good it makes you feel when someone gives you a compliment, or offers love without expecting anything in return. If your child can grow up in a home where he feels loved and wanted, he will experience a security that will allow self-confidence to grow, as well as provide him with a happy, contented disposition.

The simplicity of this book is designed as a guide to "put the shoe on the other foot". It will allow you, as parents, an insight from your baby's perspective to learn, grow and experience life together. This, in turn, will not only make your parental journey the most enjoyable, rewarding adventure you are ever likely to have, but also guide you and your baby to a happy, healthy and, most importantly, loving relationship.

*Praise will instill confidence to at least try.
Criticism will create a fear of failure.*

PRE-BORN TO DELIVERY ROOM AND BEYOND

Nine months seem like a very long time to get used to the idea of becoming a parent, but with such a lot to organize, and new experiences to endure, the time will go quickly. The exception will be the last few weeks. They seem to drag because of the physical discomfort, and knowing you are so close, but how close? The anticipation of this great event that is just around the corner is almost too much to bear, but the time will come, and your life will never be the same again.

The lead up to delivering your baby is really important. Of course, during the nine months of gestation, you will attend regular appointments with your doctor who will monitor your progress with examinations and ultra-sounds, and will guide you towards what might be expected during delivery.

Attending antenatal clinic is a very good idea, because here you will be taught how to breathe to ease the pain of a natural birth, and your partner will be shown how to massage your spine very gently to also calm the trauma your body is going through. To have someone coaching you to breathe and hold on to when the going gets serious, is a wonderful comfort in itself.

About 6–8 weeks before due date it's a very good idea to begin stimulating your nipples ready for breast feeding (if that's what you want when baby is born), because it takes time for your breasts to adjust to the need of supplying baby.

Stimulation is done by taking the nipple between the forefinger and the middle finger, (halfway between the first and second knuckles) and then firmly slide the fingers along the nipple. To avoid any discomfort, a little oil or saliva will allow the fingers to slide easier. Repeat the process several times on a daily basis.

By stimulating your breasts before baby is born, you will notice that in time an orange/yellow substance will flow from the nipple. This is known as colostrum, and is full of your antibodies, which will boost baby's immune system naturally. As stated in the introduction, mother's milk is by far the best for your baby, but sometimes breast feeding is either not possible or not desired by mother. Even if baby only receives this colostrum, it's a tremendous beginning to mother/baby bonding, and baby's health.

The actual milk doesn't "come down" for a few days after birth, but when it does; you will probably need special breast pads to stop the milk from overflowing on to your clothes. In the meantime just breast feed baby whenever he is hungry, and nature will do the rest.

Your breasts will swell considerably when the milk does come down, and it could flow too quickly for baby to swallow, which could cause excess wind or colic. If this happens, you can squeeze the breast a few times and let the milk squirt into a cloth to ease the pressure, or lay down on your back, place baby on a pillow on your stomach so the milk has to run uphill when baby is feeding. This means your milk will flow only at the pace baby can manage to suck.

Once your milk supply has settled into a pattern of what baby requires, you will find your breasts will shrink a lot. Don't worry, it doesn't mean your milk has suddenly disappeared. It's just nature's way of making things a little more comfortable for you, and you will probably be able to stop wearing the breast pads.

When breastfeeding, be aware that whatever you eat and drink, is exactly what baby is being fed, only in a different form. Some of the foods you normally eat, may cause baby to have severe wind. Even more important, always check that any medications you may have to take, are safe for both of you. Precaution is always better than cure, and a lot less painful for the whole family.

No doubt, at times during the pregnancy, you will look at your ever growing stomach and wonder how this gigantic "thing" is going to fit through that tiny vagina. Again, nature has made it very possible, and as long as there are no complications, all you have to do is bear some pain, push at the right moments, and bask in the joy of giving birth.

If any complications do arise, your medical staff will quickly change the format of what they are doing to protect you and your baby's safety.

For this reason, sometimes a natural birth can end up having to be a caesarean, and if this happens, you will be quickly prepped to go into the operating theatre.

A "C Section" or caesarean birth is a major operation, even though they are commonplace now. Modern surgery is a lot less stressful than in the past, and recovery doesn't take as long, but it is still a major trauma to your body, which means you will have some abdominal pain from being cut open and then stitched up.

Whichever way baby is born, the placenta must be removed and weighed, so with natural birth it should come away as part of the birth. With a caesarean delivery, the medical team will have to manually lift the placenta out of the womb.

Regardless, nature still has to complete her 'household' duties of cleaning out, and reprogramming the reproductive system in preparation for further pregnancies, so with natural birth, the bleeding that has occurred while giving birth will continue for up to six weeks, and with a caesarean, vaginal bleeding will begin soon after baby is delivered.

At this time, it's advisable not to use tampons, which can impede the natural flow, and maybe cause an unnecessary discomfort. Using sanitary pads will also allow you to keep a check on whether there is any abnormal discharge or blood clots, and if so, your doctor will be able to advise whether there is any need for concern.

It's this first six weeks that are very stressful in more ways than one, and the main stress is usually NO SEXUAL INTERCOURSE. The reason for this is to allow time for the vaginal stitches to dissolve (can be very painful for both parties otherwise), and to prevent any infection or unpassed blood clot being forced back into the body which could cause serious problems or even death.

After four to six weeks, and certainly after the six week check up, it's entirely up to you as a couple when sex will take place. Remember though, pregnancy can now occur again, so take precautions, even if you are breast feeding. Your doctor will recommend what pill should be taken if that's the precaution you choose.

On the other side of the coin, a comfortable session of sex can encourage baby that it's time to enter the world naturally, and this could be a far better option than having to be induced.

Doctors now don't like a patient to go more than a week to ten days past the estimated date of birth, so they will put mother-to-be in hospital and inject her with a solution that will bring on labour.

*Patience and tolerance will show me understanding.
Impatience and intolerance will lower my self esteem.*

FOR THE NEW PARENTS

As expressed in the Introduction, parenthood is something that has to be experienced to know exactly what impact it has on your life. No one can explain the overwhelming difference a baby makes to daily existence. I say "existence", because for the first 6–8 weeks at least, that's what it can all feel like.

Lack of sleep is the main reason for feeling so overwhelmed and out of control. Add to this the uncertainty of whether you are doing things correctly, not knowing why baby is crying so much, the lack of time and interest in your own romantic relationship, and the pressure of trying to have some sort of normality about your day, and you have the makings of a pretty stressful situation.

In a relationship it takes a lot of understanding, compromising, and even forgiveness for each other to make this new experience tolerable, let alone enjoyable.

The question of "why on earth did I ever want a baby" will no doubt enter your mind at some time or another when you're feeling totally depleted of sleep and energy, but take heart, your thoughts are completely normal, and during these down moments take the time to look very closely at the most beautiful creation you have achieved. Look at the innocence of this most precious little being, and know the love you have and give your baby is totally unconditional. Within a very short space of time your baby will reciprocate your love by smiling every time he hears your gentle loving voice. If you haven't already felt an overwhelming surge of love and adoration for this little bundle of yours every day since birth, you sure will when those big, beautiful, sparkling eyes look at you with the recognition that you are his mummy or daddy.

In being totally consumed by the needs of your new baby, you won't have had any time and/or interest in being the loving couple you were before the arrival of baby. For most couples this lack of interest is largely one sided from the new mum. Dad you have to be very understanding and patient about this.

Firstly, sex is usually discouraged in the initial 4–6 weeks, because the body needs time to adjust and repair from the miracle it has just taken 9 months to create. Hormone levels have to re-balance, reproductive organs have to clean out and begin a new cycle for future pregnancies, and if sexual intercourse takes place before all of this happens, you run the risk of a blood clot being pushed back into the body with the possibility of causing a heart attack. So, until the all-clear has been given, find other mutually satisfying ways of showing love for each other.

Each of you could feel they are more hardly done by than the other. Dad because you have to get up and go to work each day, and at least pretend to be wide awake and know exactly what is going on around you, but in fact you are tired, stressed, "unloved", and expected to happily want to do some domestic chore or spend time trying to settle baby when you do eventually get home from work. And you haven't had an afternoon nap like your wife has.

All you've got on your mind is coming home to a comfortable "nest" free of stress, filled with love, food, maybe a nice bottle of wine, good conversation and great sex. GET REAL—You've just had a baby. Don't panic! It can all be achieved again. Just not all at once, and probably not without interruption for some years to come. Make the most of every moment together, and even though sex is no doubt the ONLY outcome you want, show some resourcefulness by learning to turn on the dishwasher, make breakfast for two, buy a small gift, give some loving hugs and kisses WITHOUT any mention of sex; make your woman feel special, and you could be pleasantly surprised at how often satisfaction comes your way for such a small investment.

Wife can quite often believe husband has the better deal in all this, because he can at least escape to work away from the endless feeding, crying, changing of nappies, and housework that just won't do itself. He's in a position if he doesn't want to come straight home from work, he doesn't have to, and this so called freedom can sometimes set up some resentment from housebound wife.

Having a positive attitude to being a mum goes a long way to bringing harmony and happiness into your home. Don't neglect yourself because of tiredness or lack of motivation. Make the effort for yourself, because looking and feeling good will make you happier, and allow you to enjoy your day with your baby. Besides, if you don't look after yourself, how will you be able to look after the ones you love?

Should the day be filed in the 'too hard basket', for some reason, take yourself and baby out of the house to someone or somewhere you would prefer to be. Whatever is not going to plan on this day will either still be there when you come home, or it will lose its importance while you're out.

Life is not a fairy tale of living happily ever after. There is a lot of effort and understanding needed on all fronts to achieve the happiness you so wanted by having your baby.

Now, more than ever, it's a time of compromise, but keep the candles of love and lust burning between you. Life has only changed direction from the way you knew it, so willingly change with it, and enjoy what's on offer.

Unfortunately, some new mothers experience postnatal depression after the birth of their child. The extent of this condition can range from an inexplicable oversensitivity resulting in lots of tears, right through to very serious depression.

During the whole process of conception to birth, hormones experience an incredible roller coaster ride, peaking and troughing without much indication of the turmoil going on within the body.

After baby is born, the hormone levels are "dropped from a great height" instantaneously, which can cause emotional pressures not normally a part of your personality, and can take some time to level out. Crying for no apparent reason is nature's release valve to ease this sudden physical plunge, and is very common; but, if there is a sense of hopelessness, despair or any other sinister thoughts, the extent of the depression is a lot more serious

DO NOT keep this discomfort or pain a secret, because sharing it with a friend and/or your doctor could save you such a lot of needless unhappiness. Postnatal depression is well recognized nowadays, and help is at hand either through the normal medical channels or alternative means, and by doing something about it quickly, means you will be able to enjoy life and baby to the fullest.

Discipline will give me secure boundaries to grow in.
Unregulated freedom will make me insecure and uncertain.

NEWBORN

CONGRATULATIONS!

I'm the precious cargo you've been carrying around for the last nine months, and as these months have passed, I have developed into a little human being. My beginnings have been in a small, noisy oven at a constant temperature of 37.5oC, but it has been a very secure, warm environment, and, believe it or not, educational too.

In a perfect world, it could be mummy, daddy and baby makes three, but I know that isn't always the way things are; and at this time, it isn't important to me whether you're young, old, married, single, rich or poor, or come from outer space. Maybe when I'm older, the fact that I have two mums or dads, instead of one of each, or maybe that you are a single parent could be of importance, but at this time, all I need is love and attention.

I know you're crying because you're so happy I'm finally here—your little miracle. I know you couldn't wait for me to be born to bring happiness to our family, and I will certainly do just that, but you have to understand that I am going to make you very tired and your routine will now no longer exist as you have known it. There will be times when you become very short tempered with me and with each other, because it will seem as though you do nothing else but look after me. I am a very high maintenance little package, who needs a lot of TLC, regardless of how tired you are or what other commitments you have. But, I am also the cuddliest, most valuable and beautiful gift you will ever receive.

For 9 months, while I was developing, I got to know you. I recognize your voice, your smell, and now your touch and I can sense when you're calm or when you're anxious. Being in a peaceful, loving environment is much better for me than a home full of tension with loud yelling and screaming, and although I am only a baby, I'm very sensitive to my surroundings, and will react quickly to any sudden changes or loud noises. That reaction will probably be for me to cry, which will no doubt make you more anxious, and the whole situation pretty unpleasant.

While we are in hospital, I will be kept very comfortable, dressed in singlet, nappy, booties, mittens and jumpsuit, and maybe even a jacket; then wrapped tightly in a lovely soft blanket that covers the back of my head. This helps me get used to the freedom of not being restricted in the womb anymore, and gives me a sense of security while I adjust to being newborn.

Now that the hype and excitement of my birth has died down, you could feel a little unsure about suddenly becoming a parent. Don't worry, it's quite normal with all those hormones racing around, and the special attention we're both getting.

Whether we are in a private room or sharing with other mums and babies, my crib will most likely be in your room, and this will allow you to get to know my feeding and sleeping patterns.

Now that I'm out in the big wide world, my body also has some adjustments to make. This means that the build up of fluids and mucus from being in your womb, need to be expelled so my organs can function properly, therefore, my motions (or dirty nappies) are going to be very slimy and different colours. If you have any doubts or problems concerning either of us, the nursing staff is on duty 24 hours a day, and will gladly answer all your questions, or even show you how to do something you're not sure of.

Don't ever hesitate to ask for assistance, because we both want life to be as enjoyable and hassle free as possible.

Encouragement will give me the confidence to explore and experience.
Discouragement will make me fearful of new experiences.

IT'S TIME TO GO HOME

Being such a precious passenger, you will make sure I am harnessed into my capsule properly with another blanket over me snug as a bug. Of course, if it's a very hot day, I won't need all those clothes and blankets, but a very light blanket may be a good idea, especially if you have a strong air conditioner turned on in the car. Do protect me from the Sun. That is definitely no good for my delicate skin.

*Respect will increase all my values.
Disrespect is soul destroying.*

HOME AT LAST

I'm sorry I'm crying, but my tummy is very small and I get hungry lots of times during the day and night, so feeding me on demand is probably best for all of us at this point in time.

If I keep crying after you feed me, it could be because:

I have wind and need to be burped

Put me over your shoulder, and rub or pat my back, or sit me up with your hand under my chin as explained in the "Helpful Hints" page.

I have a wet or dirty nappy

For a wet nappy, simply change to a clean dry one. If I have a dirty nappy, I need you to wipe my bottom clean and then put a nice clean nappy on.

I am hot or cold (usually cold)

Just ensure I am dressed appropriately for the weather conditions. If cool, make sure my feet, hands and head are covered.

Because I make a lot of noises when I sleep, it's much better for you if we don't sleep in the same room. Nature has made it possible for you to sleep soundly, and just instinctively know to wake up when I need you. For reassurance, buy and use a baby monitor. At least then you have control over the volume of my noises.

During the next 6–8 weeks all I'll want to do is eat, sleep, fill my nappies and have a nice warm bath nearly every day. In this time you will see that I have grown quite a lot, because that's what happens while I sleep.

I'm not much fun yet, but I love hearing you talk softly to me, telling me how much you love me and how special I am to you, even though you probably feel like giving me away, because I've made you so tired.

Having lived in fluid for 9 months, I really like my nice warm bath with your hand or arm behind my head for support so I don't slide into the water. My bath time doesn't have to be very long at first; it's just to freshen me up and make me comfortable for bed. A few drops of lavender oil in my bath water can have a calming effect that will help put me to sleep.

When you put me in my crib, please don't lay me on my tummy, because I'm too young to be able to lift my head or turn over, and I might suffocate. Lay me on my side or back, and tuck me in tightly. My head is still very soft, so if you put me on the same side all the time, I will have a dented head. I don't need a pillow yet, and make sure there isn't one just for decoration in my crib that might fall on my head or over my face.

While I was in your tummy, I sucked my thumb. Perhaps you don't want me to suck my thumb now, so to pacify me, you may prefer I suck a dummy. It was also very noisy in there and I could hear your heartbeat, but it's very quiet in my new home, so maybe a ticking clock placed under my mattress will make me think it is your heartbeat. I also know there are CDs you can buy with noises I am used to that might help me go to sleep. The other alternative is to play classical music (Mozart), sounds of nature, or some other calming sounds which will relax both of us.

Until I am about one year old, try not to let anyone kiss me on the mouth. Adults, other than my mummy, can easily transmit germs that my immune system is not able to cope with, and this precaution could save me from being unnecessarily sick. A gentle kiss on the top of my head or forehead is all I need.

Guidance will create a safe path, and avoid unnecessary mistakes.
Lack of guidance will result in ignorance.

OUR FIRST OUTING

Snuggle me safe and sound into my capsule. Make sure you have clean nappies, a blanket and even a change of clothes, and bottles of formula already made up in case we are out longer than you think.

Until you get used to taking me with you, it might be a good idea for you to make a checklist of the things we may need while we're out.

I know you're warm in your short sleeves and sandals, but I am still very small and my body cannot hold its temperature like yours, so I need to be dressed warmer than you. Again, remember that I feel the effects of air conditioning much more than you.

You know how you feel cold when you lie down because your blood flow slows, well I'm like that all the time because I'm not active yet. My head, fingers and toes get cold very easily if they are not covered, and that could be the reason why I'm crying. I AM COLD! I know I look cute in my little jumpsuit, but it doesn't offer me much warmth.

One of our first outings will be to the health centre to check my weight, height, head measurement, and all sorts of other things including whether I'm feeding well, sleeping soundly, suffering from wind, and a general checkup of how my umbilical cord is healing.

The health centre sister is a lovely person who will contact you after you come out of hospital, and who can answer lots of questions to make you feel more comfortable that you're doing everything right for me. She will also be able to advise you if something is wrong and I need to be taken to the doctor, as well as let you know where and when to take me for my immunizations against all those nasty diseases.

She will also tell you about the mothers' group in our neighborhood.

All the ladies in the group are the same as you. Some mums will have more than one baby, but it's nice for you to meet and make friends with them, so you have someone in the same situation that you can talk to. Lot's of times a lasting friendship will be formed with someone in the group, and that means I will have a play mate to grow up with too.

I'm too young to understand any benefit I will get from socializing yet, but as I get older, interaction with other children is a vital part of my learning experience. Besides, if you enjoy talking to these ladies, it means you will feel happy and I like that.

*Trust builds self-esteem to make decisions.
Distrust creates reasons for dishonesty.*

BABY NOT NEWBORN

Now I'm about 8 weeks old, I can stay awake for longer periods of time to kick without my nappy on, and play with the rattle that I can now sort of hold.

As well as staying awake longer, I should also be sleeping longer between feeds, especially at night, but there will be times when I need an extra feed to compensate for lots of dirty nappies or throwing up, or even a growth spurt.

I am also old enough now to lie on my tummy on the floor with a blanket under me.

Two reasons for the blanket—it's more comfortable and hygienic for me, and if I throw up, the mess will be less trouble for you on the blanket than on the carpet.

Lying on the floor like this will make me try and lift my head, which will make my neck stronger. It will also allow me to move my arms and legs differently which, again, will make my limbs stronger. All this exercise is getting me ready to be able to sit up, then crawl and then walk.

Doing this straight after a feed is not a good idea, because all my weight is balanced on my tummy which means I will probably throw up.

Between now and 3 months I will have grown quite a lot so I am able to sleep about 8 hours during the night from 10pm to 6am, but after my morning feed and nappy change, I will probably want to go back to sleep again.

Because I am stronger now, I can sit up as long as I have lots of pillows around me, but be careful I am still very much like a rag doll, and will probably fall to the side on my face. Smiling and goo garring are also things I can do now, especially hearing your voice and seeing your smiling face. It's all part of the bond we have between us. You greet me with a loving "good morning" or whatever and I'll give you the biggest smile I can find. That makes you want to cuddle and kiss me, and so no matter what sort of a sleepless night we had, our new day starts off in a positive, loving way, and will hopefully continue happily from there.

FOUR–SIX MONTHS

By the age of 4–6 months a lot of things are taking place.

I stay awake longer, so now I may only need three sleeps a day.

I have been introduced to that special breakfast cereal (usually a rice cereal called Farax) mixed with my milk or boiled water.

I have also tasted those mushy vegetables (mashed potato/pumpkin) that you cook specially for me without any salt or flavourings.

Formula is not the same as breast milk. It doesn't contain the complete balance of nutrients that I need, so you should have introduced me to water by now, particularly if we are in the summer months. To kill any harmful germs, it's important that my water is boiled. It can then be stored in an airtight container or my bottle in the fridge. But, before giving it to me, make sure the water is about the same warm temperature as my milk.

It will take time for me to get used to the different flavour and texture of water, because it is so different from my milk, so I'm likely to cough and splutter.

Don't be put off though. My little body needs water to stop dehydration, and besides, I get thirsty just like you. I will eventually enjoy my drink of water. Don't force me to drink or eat anything—it's only about introducing me to different foods at this stage, and even just a mouthful is plenty.

TEETHING

Sitting up is fun (except for the times when I fall over). I love holding onto my rattles especially the ones I can chew on, because my teeth are starting to grow which makes my gums really sore until they pop through and you can see them. Who knows? I might even have one or two teeth already.

Because it hurts while my teeth are growing, I will probably be unhappy and cry a lot more than usual. I might not want to eat much, my nose could be runny, my temperature could be higher than normal with an earache or chest infection, my cheeks are probably rosy red, and my nappies could smell like dead fish. I will more than likely also get bad nappy rash.

It's all very wearing for you too. Just comfort and cuddle me. Take me for a walk. Sing to me. Read to me, or take me for a drive. Maybe we could go and visit a close friend or Grandma, who will give you moral support while you have coffee and a chat. If we are at Grandma's house, she could take me for a walk or something while you lie down and have a rest.

If 'things' are all too much to handle, maybe Grandma could come and stay with us for a few days so she can help us get settled again, or we could go stay at her house. Maybe daddy could have a few days off work, and we could all be 'miserable' together. Whatever happens, just know it won't last forever.

Depending on how big I am, it's probably time to start letting me sleep in my cot. This change is going to be a big one for me because I'm used to being tucked tightly in my bassinette without very much room to move. The cot to me will be like you sleeping in a single bed and then changing to a king-size—lots more room. Unlike you, I won't stay facing the right way up. I will wriggle out of my blankets and turn around all different ways. You will have to keep checking on me and covering me up so I don't get cold or caught up in my blankets. There is a 'wedge' you can buy that can be placed in my cot which is designed to keep me snug and "in place".

My cot needs to have a nice warm blanket or overlay on the mattress and under the sheet. A cloth nappy under my head is a good idea in case I'm sick, and it's warmer for me to lie on. When I'm a little bit older, I can lay on a really thin pillow. For winter, flannelette sheets are cozy for me, and a sleeping bag is also a really good idea, because when I wriggle out of my blankets, the sleeping bag will keep me quite warm.

A portacot is extremely useful for when we are out visiting and it's nap time, because you can enjoy yourself without having to either nurse me or worry whether I'll fall off the bed. Even at this young age don't trust me to sleep on a bed without pillows around me to safeguard against an unwanted fall.

*Independence encourages strength and reliability.
Dependence is crippling to growth.*

SEVEN-NINE MONTHS

I have already learnt such a lot, but between now and the time I turn 1 year old, I have lots of different things to learn.

When you put me on my tummy now, I will be trying to crawl. Maybe I have already found a way of moving about, so you will have to make sure that our home is safe for my exploring. I will like to pull at things even though I don't know what they are, so hopefully it won't hurt me if it falls on me. Everything I pick up will no doubt end up in my mouth because I have no idea that some things could make me sick or hurt me.

I love all my toys that are brightly coloured, make a noise and move in different directions, especially when you play with me and make them work properly. By now I can recognize a lot of pictures like animals and stars, flowers and the moon, so the more you tell and ask me what these things are, the sooner I will be able to tell you.

I'm beginning to understand a lot of what you say to me, but of course I still can't talk so it might seem to you that I don't know what you're saying yet. It's probably better for my development now if there is no more 'baby talk'. Speaking to me using normal words could save a lot of confusion when I do begin to talk. Of course, I won't have the ability to pronounce the words properly, but at least my brain will have received the correct message.

I know exactly when you're happy or sad and whether you think I'm good or naughty. I can tell by your voice and the look on your face. I hate it when you're angry because you think I have done something naughty. I haven't meant to spill my drink. I'm still learning how to hold my hands around the cup, tip it up just enough to get the right amount into my mouth and hold my balance at the same time.

This learning experience is called co-ordination and development of motor skills, and will take me quite some time to master. So if I do muck up, I like it much better when you say "never mind, it was just an accident". Maybe I could help you to clean up the mess, and I promise I will try harder next time.

10–12 MONTHS OLD

I'm a little person now who can walk around holding on to the furniture, bend down, make some of my toys work, and look at my books all by myself. I am showing some independence, but you probably still think I'm a baby who doesn't know anything and can't do much. Guess what! I can say a few words like mum mum and dad dad, and I understand so much of what you're saying. I recognize a lot of things you have pointed out to me in the last year, and I will be trying to tell you what they are. It will be in baby talk, but you'll know what I'm saying. I need you to encourage me. Keep telling me how clever I am. Clap your hands and smile at me. Be excited, and these reactions will make me want to try even harder, because I love it when I've got your attention.

There are times when I make you very angry for some reason. I don't mean to make you angry or sad. Physically hurting me will only make me cry, and that will make you angrier, so being patient and explaining is better for both of us.

It probably seems silly to you, but explaining every little detail of your actions to me, will help me understand the meaning of patience. For instance, I want some apple. Tell me I may have a piece of apple as soon as you have peeled it, and I will learn to stand quietly while you prepare it for me.

There will be times when my request is definitely not on. Perhaps I want the knife you're using to peel my apple, so again, by explaining in detail that there is a danger I might hurt myself should deter me from wanting it. My immediate reaction may be a typical childlike tantrum, but with consistent explanation, and some authority in your voice, I will soon learn the lesson.

I wasn't born knowing what love and hatred, fear and confidence, or right and wrong are, so you have to teach me. I need you to show me love, and give me security, encouragement and praise.

If you keep telling me how bad I am, and yelling at me, or smacking me all the time, you are making me believe you don't love me, because I'm not worthy of being loved. Being nasty and negative towards me instead of loving and positive could make me even naughtier. I need your attention, so if being naughty is the only way I can get it, then that's what I'll do.

I know we can't play together all the time. You need to do things without me hanging off you, and I need to entertain myself to learn the value of my own thoughts and company, as well as being educated and stimulated by my books, toys and television.

Television has some wonderful programs for kids of all ages. Encourage me to watch Playschool, Sesame Street, or Hi 5. My initial attention span will only be short, but in time I'll watch the whole program. These types of programs are really good for kids because they have music, colour, repetition, movement and these will help me to develop coordination and memory. Remember that girls are usually quicker to learn than boys at this age. It isn't good for me to sit in front of television too much though.

My feeding has changed a lot by now. I have breakfast, lunch and dinner just like you, but earlier than you. Please don't make me wait until you have your meals, because my tummy can't wait that long, and it would interfere with my sleeping schedule. In between meals, a healthy snack of fruit and lots of water to drink are much better for me than sweets and soft drink. It's likely I still have a bottle before I go to bed, but now it's not nearly as important to my diet as it was before I was able to eat solid food.

There are some things that I can't or don't want to eat, and because I don't have all my teeth yet, chewing some things is still too hard. My taste buds have developed so I am getting to know what I like and what I don't like. Maybe it's not your idea of a good balanced diet, but please don't force me to eat if I don't want to. I have a very good reason why I don't want something. I just can't tell you yet. If there is fresh food in our house, I won't starve.

If I'm bottle fed, it's time to stop giving me formula, and gradually introduce me to cow's milk. It has to be full cream milk though, not light or skinny because I need all the nutrients contained in full cream milk to ensure healthy growth. There is a possibility I am allergic to cow's milk, so look for signs such as vomiting, diarrhea, rash, etc. that may indicate this, and seek advice from the Health Centre Sister or Doctor.

Some mothers are now choosing to completely stop any form of milk intake at this stage, because studies have shown milk may not necessarily be an integral part of my diet after the first year.

Should you decide to introduce me to another sort of milk, such as soy or cow's milk, after weaning me off my formula, do not, under any circumstances, flavour it with things like topping or Milo. My body can't process the excess sugar in these artificial flavourings, and may cause health problems when I'm older.

Solid food is now more important to my development than milk, so I should be encouraged to eat before having my bottle of milk.

My immune system is a lot stronger now, and my body can deal with some of the germs that I swallow, but please keep things I use and play with as clean as you can. You don't have to sterilize my bottles any more either, but they must be washed and rinsed very well in hot water.

Your home cooked meals are much better for me than bottled or canned food, but there will be times when it is easier to feed me with something bought, and that's okay, but just be careful what you're feeding me.

Food, suitable for babies of my age can be bought at supermarkets, but be aware of the sugar, salt and preservative content on the label.

*Equality prevents unfair judgment.
Inequality harbours resentment and injustice.*

1–2 YEARS OLD

Walking is easy as pie and I can even run. I can throw a ball, dance to music, clap my hands, draw on paper (and walls), feed myself and hold my own cup of water. I probably still can't drink from a straw yet.

I know extremely well the words YES and NO, and I can answer simple questions. I have long conversations with you; unfortunately you don't speak my language. It doesn't matter that you don't understand me; I'm just practicing what I have to do with my tongue and mouth to be able to talk properly.

Sometimes I could throw a tantrum for no reason. Maybe I'm tired or sick of sitting in my pusher or supermarket trolley. Perhaps I'm hungry or thirsty. Whatever the reason, yelling at me will only make me worse. Throwing my food on the floor is not what you want to see, but for some reason, every kid does it sometime. Sure, tell me what I have done is naughty and take it away. I obviously don't want to eat. Don't place too much importance on any of it, and I will eventually realize it's not getting me any special attention so what's the point.

I still really don't know what fear is, but I am becoming aware of a natural caution towards people and things I don't know all that well. Forcing me to overcome this shyness will only make the situation worse, so leave me alone and I will come around when I feel comfortable and secure enough.

My personality has developed quite noticeably. If I have been given lots of love and guidance since I was born, I will be a happy, funny little character with loads of energy and always looking for things to occupy me. I love playing with you, but I can also play by myself. Sometimes my games are very messy like when I pull all the saucepans or plastics out of the cupboards. Don't worry I'm having a lot of harmless fun. It could get very messy though if you leave the food cupboard open.

Crying is still really the only way I have of telling you I'm unhappy for some reason. By now you will know my different cries. I have a serious one with real tears that comes from the heart because I need you. Just wanting my own way will be a half hearted noise and screwed up face or maybe even a full blown tantrum. Although, if I am sick, I'm more likely to be very quiet and lethargic, with no interest in anything but possibly sleeping.

When it's just wanting my own way, I need you to be strong and don't give in to what I want if there is a very good reason why you shouldn't. You see I'm old enough now to understand a little bit of what discipline is. I don't like it, but I need to be taught I can't have my own way all the time. If you don't teach me this, I will become selfish, as well as very demanding, and not respect that you mean what you say. I will also learn that I can manipulate you, and you won't carry out the discipline you have set out. That's another good reason to only warn me with some punishment you can and will carry out if I won't behave. I need boundaries to grow in so I don't try to grow up too quickly. I'm not capable of making my own decisions yet, so I need your guidance. Things can become too complicated for me if I have too many choices. Two options at once are plenty for me, and sometimes it's better if there is no choice.

I really like climbing. You know I could fall and hurt myself, but if you keep a close watch on me, no harm will come to me. It's just another experience that every kid needs to help develop strength, balance and co-ordination. Encouraging and calmly guiding me on how to climb will have me confidently doing it in no time at all. A time saver for you at meal times, etc. Just be careful though. The next step is dragging the chair over to the bench, sink, or stove to 'help my mummy', and that can set up a very dangerous situation.

There are times when I will try your patience to the limit, but don't worry; it's just a phase, and besides, the terrible twos are on their way; as well as those horrible two year old molars. It may appear that my good behaviour and logical reasoning have deserted me, but be assured, they will surface again when I'm a little older.

THE ARRIVAL OF A SIBLING

What's a baby brother or sister? How come it's in your tummy? How am I supposed to love it when I don't even know what it is? You're excited about it, so I guess it must be something good. During the next 7–8 months you will have to keep reminding me that a new baby is something to look forward to, and I'm going to love it too.

When my baby brother or sister arrives, everyone will give it presents and all their attention. Don't forget to make me feel special too. I've had your complete attention for about 2 years, and I'm not used to having to share you with a squashed up, noisy little blob. Talk to me. Reassure me that you love me just as much as you did before, and that you haven't really given me to nanny and pop because you have a new baby.

I don't understand why you have to spend so much time with this baby so my demands could be a little unreasonable, and I might do silly things. Anything, to get your attention. I'm jealous! I don't like this new competition.

If I am misbehaving, while you're feeding my new brother or sister, maybe you could encourage me to read a book or play with a toy. Perhaps we could talk or sing together, and then I might not feel left out.

2–3 YEARS OLD

Now I'm getting bigger, I can have conversations with you. I am able to put little sentences together and answer questions with more than one word.

I'm still a mischief exploring what's in cupboards and drawers, and I love pulling stuff out for no reason. I know I have a lot of lovely toys, but sometimes I like a change so I'll play with the plastic containers I spilled all over the floor, or climb in and out of the cupboard I just emptied. A little bit of coaxing in the way of a game, (who can put the most back?) will be the beginning of me understanding tidiness. There will be days though that nothing will make me put things back. It's all part of my learning curve and development of my personality. Remember we all have bad days, and I'm here to test your patience to its limit—or so it seems.

My coordination is heaps better now, so I like to throw or kick the ball. I can put shapes into their right place. Some of that comes from remembering and some by accident. Whichever it might be, praise me for being so clever which will make me keep trying to do things better, and not afraid to try new things. I remember so much, like songs I've heard over and over, and I can sing some of them too.

During the last 2–3 years all that boring repetition of reading, pointing the same things out and singing the same songs again and again have been stored in my memory bank, and I am very proud to show you how I have remembered all that information.

TOILET TRAINING

Toilet training is like everything else I've learnt so far. I won't get it right immediately. Even though it's not comfortable, I'm still not really able to understand why I can't just continue to do everything in my nappy. Potty training may be less frightening for me than sitting on the toilet, but no less frustrating for you. For some reason learning to do wee is a lot easier than poo, so all the encouragement you can muster will help me understand this new activity quicker.

I will have accidents. Overlook them, play them down, don't get angry, because your anger will only make me very self-conscious and not want to try. Also, making me sit on the potty for a long time will only make me think it is a punishment rather than a normal function.

Speaking of toilets: I will have been following you around like a little puppy dog for as long as I have been able to crawl, and of course that means into the bathroom when you go to the toilet. There will be times when I may want to sit on your knee. It isn't the private time you had in mind, especially if it's "that time of the month" when I could be quite horrified that you're bleeding. Just treat the whole process as normal, and reassure me that you are perfectly alright. Within a space of time, I'll accept that. By being open and honest with me from such an early age, will allow me a lot more understanding of bodily functions as I grow older, and it doesn't matter whether I'm a boy or a girl. I'll grow out of this habit long before you feel embarrassed by my presence, but it's still a really good idea to let me know where you're going so I don't get a fright if I can't see or hear you.

Remember the mothers' group? Maybe we still take part in those days or maybe we go to play group. It's very important that during my first few years, I get used to the company of other children while you're nearby. This will give me a lot of confidence to develop social skills with other kids in preparation to go to kindergarten all by myself.

My first three years have been all about learning, and most of that has come from you, my parents. It's very important that you both share similar ideas on how to support, encourage, discipline, and educate me. That way I will learn to respect, trust and obey you without fear of any repercussion.

A united front from both of you is the only way discipline will work. If one of you tells me off, or disciplines me in some way, it is important that the other doesn't try to pacify me, because I will just learn to play you against each other to get my own way. Simplicity and consistency is the key to achieving the harmony we want in our family.

I have learnt things you can see like crawling, walking and jumping, but I have also learnt so many things that you can't see, and because these make up a large portion of what my character is, and will be, they are probably more important.

I have learnt the difference between:	Like and dislike
	Happy and sad
	Security and insecurity
	Fun and serious
	Obedience and disobedience
	Praise and criticism
	Positive and negative
	Calm and anxiety

No. I can't explain them and I don't really understand most of them, but they are all part of my development. Hopefully your guidance is towards all the positives, and while you're teaching me right from wrong, it's in a way that won't harm my self-esteem.

It doesn't matter if you have to work and I'm left in child care, or at home with a nanny, my basic need is still your love and attention. There is absolutely no material object you can buy me that is more valuable to my upbringing, than your time.

I will be the best kid I can possibly be, because you are teaching me to believe in myself, and I am so looking forward to celebrating my third birthday.

CONCLUSION

When a baby is born, there is really nothing more innocent, pure and precious in this World, having been safely protected in the womb for its nine months of gestation. It's this purity of life that we, as adults, have full control over, and should nurture with all our might to ensure a happy, healthy life is the final outcome.

Perhaps your own childhood wasn't as you would have liked it; then it will be easy for you to relate to what this book is about. In all situations imagine you are the child. What would you want your parent to say or do in the same circumstances. I believe the choice would always be a positive reaction or explanation.

If you love and respect yourself, you won't have a problem passing that confidence on to your child, but so many adults don't have that attribute, and feel that they can't teach something they don't have. Wrong! It's a matter of recognizing that a positive attitude or input, results in achievement, and a negative attitude or input is just totally destructive.

Children are our future, so if we can 'mould' them into self-respecting, compassionate and caring people, future generations may learn to co-exist, and live peacefully on our beautiful planet.

HELPFUL HINTS

Breast milk is made to order for baby's every need, but if not possible, a bottle of formula is fine too. Be aware that baby could be lactose intolerant, and therefore may require a special formula mixture.

Bottles need to be sterilized very carefully when baby is young to avoid any contamination, and water used to make the formula needs to have been boiled too. Sterilizers can be bought from an electrical store, or using a pot of boiling water on the cook top works equally as well. Antibacterial liquid can be bought and added to the water if you desire.

Make up the formula using cold—warm boiled water. It's much quicker and easier to make up the whole day's requirements at once, and store in the fridge until needed.

Before feeding, test the temperature of the formula by squirting a few drops on the underside of your arm. If you can hardly feel it against your skin, the temperature is suitable for baby.

To test the temperature of baby's bathwater, dip your elbow into the water. Again, if you can hardly feel it against your skin, it will be suitable for baby.

A warm cloth to wash baby's bottom is much more comfortable than those freezing cold wipes you buy. The wipes are a lot less trouble for you, but the coldness of the commercially made wipes is like an electric shock to baby's system.

Baby must be burped until he is approximately 4–6 months old. For the very young baby, sit him upright on your knee, place your open hand under his chin, thumb under one ear, middle finger under the other, gently stretch chin out and up, then pat or rub his back. Burping about half way through a feed will assist baby's digestion, and could help prevent colic.

Rice cereal is the only recommended 'solid' to give baby before the age of 6 months, because his digestive system is not developed enough to cope with anything heavier.

Cook enough vegetables (mashed or blended) to fill an ice cube tray. Cover with glad wrap and take cubes out for reheating when required. Simplicity is the key to starting baby on solids. Begin with vegetables such as potato and pumpkin mashed together. Don't add any salt or butter. The flavour to you is probably yuk, but remember, baby's taste buds are only used to milk. Additives are not good for baby at this time. The important thing is to get baby used to different textures. As baby eats more, the same can be done in small containers. Flavours can be changed by adding a small amount of blended lean meat and/or gravy from your dinner.

Stew pears, peaches, or apples and treat them the same as the vegetables. These can be served with custard, and make a very nutritious lunch or dinner. It isn't wise to serve baby acidic fruits or vegetables yet, because the digestive system isn't strong enough to deal with them. The result could be a very severe case of wind at least.

Baby may find a dummy soothing, especially if you don't want him to suck his fingers, and particularly when teething. A teething ring cooled in the fridge helps ease the pain. A stick of peeled (no strings) celery or a finger of cucumber (no seeds) can also ease teething pain. Watch carefully that baby doesn't manage to break off a piece too big to swallow.

Don't tell your child he is naughty or bad for something he has done, but rather what he has done is naughty. This teaches your child right from wrong without harm to his self esteem

When the new baby arrives, jealousy can occur. A way of overcoming this is to buy a small gift for your firstborn from his new baby brother or sister.

Jealousy can be a very serious problem from the point of view of a beloved dog. If your pet has been allowed to share your home indoors, and has been "spoilt rotten", don't be cruel and throw the pet outside when baby arrives home. All you will achieve is confusing the animal because it will feel it is being punished—for what?—which, in turn, could result in a natural attack on "the intruder". Allow your dog the same place in your life and safely introduce baby and dog to each other. Begin by talking to the dog about your new baby when you're pregnant, and instead of being a danger, your dog will become baby's protector. NEVER, NEVER, leave baby alone with the dog no matter how much you trust your pet, and always be very close by if the two are together.

CHILDHOOD AILMENTS

COLIC—A very painful, deep seated wind that causes baby to double up and scream.

A warm bath may help to ease the pain. Lay baby across your knees face down, and gently massage his lower back. Warm boiled water can sometimes assist. Raise the head of the bassinette so baby is not lying flat. The Doctor or health centre sister may suggest a commercial mixture from the chemist.

COMMON COLD—Nature's way of removing toxins from our bodies. Coughing, blocked up nose (which will interfere with sleeping).

White or clear mucus is harmless. Yellow mucus means it is stale. Green mucus signifies that there is a bacterial infection and may need medication. See your doctor.

It is important that baby has as much water as he will drink.

CRADLE CAP—A thick dandruff like coating on baby's head. Gently rub oil on scalp, but do not scratch the cradle cap off.

BRONCHITIS—A chest infection often the result of what appears to be the common cold.

  A visit to the doctor is necessary, especially because baby has probably got a temperature and will dehydrate quickly.

FEVER—To help bring baby's temperature down, a cool (not cold) cloth or bath and lighter clothing and blankets will assist.

GASTROENTERITIS—A stomach bug that causes throwing up and very runny bowel movements.

  Not wise to feed baby full strength formula or solid food, but as much boiled water as he will drink.

  Again a visit to the doctor is necessary to avoid dehydration, and determine whether medication is necessary.

NAPPY RASH red and sometimes blistered bottom.

  Protecting baby's bottom with Vaseline or one of the products on the market is about all you can do.

THRUSH—A fungal infection that is white in colour. This can also occur in baby's mouth.

Doctor's advice could be needed, although there are 'over the counter' products now that can be purchased and successfully treat the complaint.

AUTHOR BIOGRAPHY

My childhood dream was to grow up, get married, have children and live happily ever after. The emphasis was on being a mother, because the whole scenario of motherhood was depicted as the epitome of life's experiences.

I didn't ever lose that desire, although through my developing years, naturally, there were other priorities.

My first introduction to 'standing on my own two feet', at the age of 4, was being taken to school one day, and my mother leaving me in a place I had never been to before, amid a sea of strange faces, and with an insecurity so frightening, for the first week, I ran 3 kilometers to the sanctuary of my home. Unfortunately, my mother's response was as stern as my teacher's, and although I was never smacked, the feeling of being criticized by the people I needed encouragement and reassurance from, was probably more painful than any physical punishment. Therefore, I quickly learnt that staying at school was my only option, particularly that the "wicked witch" headmistress guarded the gate each day. With a shy and introverted personality, I moderately excelled at school and successfully completed Year 11, or what was then Leaving Certificate, with subjects suitable for secretarial work.

So at the tender age of 15, I began my first job as Secretary in the office of a newly established, secondary school, in a small country town in Gippsland, Victoria. While delighted with being appointed to the first job I had ever applied for, I still lacked confidence. This resulted in my first panic attack at the age of 16, with anxiety then becoming a major influence in my daily life.

My first child was conceived, and arrived in the midst of such personal anxiety, that the end result was a baby who, constantly cried night and day for four and a half years, with a mother suffering post natal depression in absolute silence (for fear of condemnation).

With some professional help, and great determination that this nightmare was going to end, my other two children were spared much of this emotional trauma. It was then I began to realize that following the somewhat popular trend of raising children as though they were a burden, and not worthy of consideration, was definitely not what I wanted for my beautiful children.

The wooden spoon was banished to the drawer, the loud, merciless voice became softer, and understanding took the place of intolerance. I embarked on the path to give my children confidence and balance. Sure I made mistakes, but they are now three wonderful adults and I am proud to say my very best friends, who do have strength of character and welcome me to share their lives.

My daughter's capability in her position as a nanny, and now a mother, inspired me to write this book, and share some ideas that may help to make your life as a parent that little bit easier, and much more enjoyable.

Watching my two young granddaughters happily growing, not only in size, but in confidence and manners, with an understanding of family values is the icing on my cake. This is a second chance for me to see how love and encouragement achieves so much more than negativity and power trips.

GIVEN THE CHANCE, I WOULD DO IT ALL OVER AGAIN, (With a few changes, of course).

978-0-595-42051-3
0-595-42051-6

LaVergne, TN USA
28 March 2010
177404LV00001B/33/A